BIO
CHU

Vander Hook, ☑ P9-EME-926

Winston Churchill :
British prime minister &
statesman

DATE DUE

APR 13 '12			

WINSTON

CHURCHILL

Essential Lives

WINSTON CHURCHILL

BRITISH PRIME MINISTER & STATESMAN

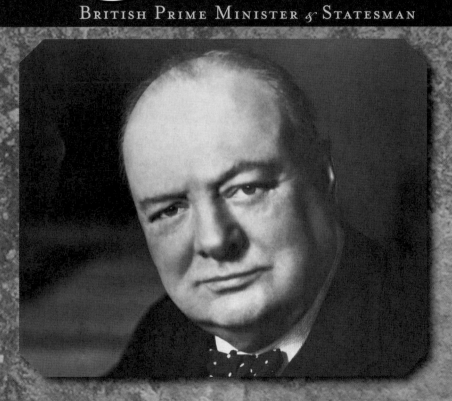

by Sue Vander Hook

Content Consultant:
Mark Blitz, PhD, Professor of Government
Claremont McKenna College

ABDO
Publishing Company

CREDITS

Published by ABDO Publishing Company, 8000 West 78th Street, Edina, Minnesota 55439. Copyright © 2009 by Abdo Consulting Group, Inc. International copyrights reserved in all countries. No part of this book may be reproduced in any form without written permission from the publisher. The Essential Library™ is a trademark and logo of ABDO Publishing Company.

Printed in the United States.

Editor: Rebecca Rowell
Copy Editor: Paula Lewis
Interior Design and Production: Nicole Brecke
Cover Design: Nicole Brecke

Library of Congress Cataloging-in-Publication Data
Vander Hook, Sue, 1949-
  Winston Churchill : British prime minister & statesman / by Sue Vander Hook.
    p. cm. — (Essential lives)
  Includes bibliographical references and index.
  ISBN 978-1-60453-523-5
  1. Churchill, Winston, Sir, 1874-1965—Juvenile literature. 2. Great Britain—Politics and government—20th century—Juvenile literature. 3. Prime ministers--Great Britain—Biography—Juvenile literature. 4. World War, 1939-1945—Great Britain—Juvenile literature. I. Title.

  DA566.9.C5V36 2009
  941.084'092—dc22
  [B]
                              2008033503

TABLE OF CONTENTS

Winston Churchill was a powerful, forthright speaker. In the 1930s, he warned the world about Adolf Hitler and Germany.

PROPHET OF TRUTH

*I*n the years leading up to World War II, Winston Churchill warned the world about Germany. He said to watch out for the National Socialist Party—the Nazis—and Adolf Hitler, Germany's leader. In a November 1932 speech, Churchill proclaimed:

> *All these bands of sturdy Teutonic [Germanic] youths . . . are not looking for status. They are looking for weapons, and, when they have the weapons, believe me they will then ask for the return of lost territories . . . it cannot fail to shake and possibly shatter to their foundations of every one of the countries [Europe] I have mentioned.*[1]

BEWARE OF HITLER

Alerting the world about Hitler and Germany became Churchill's passion and mission in the 1930s. He repeatedly pointed out Germany's rearmament and the danger this posed to Europe and the world. In a 1934 broadcast, he boldly stated that Britain was no longer safe from the Germans who were taught war and conquest from childhood. Death in battle was their noblest fate.

Tell the Truth

In addition to speaking about German youth in November 1932, Churchill discussed how politicians were not being truthful about Germany and other countries, saying, "I cannot recall any time when the gap between the kind of words which statesmen used and what was actually happening in many countries was so great as it is now. The habit of saying smooth things . . . to gain applause without relation to the underlying facts, is more pronounced now than it has ever been in my experience . . . so I would now say, 'Tell the truth to the British people.' They are a tough people. . . . They may be a bit offended at the moment, but if you have told them exactly what is going on you have insured yourself against complaints and reproaches which are very unpleasant when they come home on the morrow of some disillusion."[2]

In political circles, Churchill essentially stood alone in his beliefs, and his warnings about Germany were largely unheeded. He had little influence in the British government at that time, and most Britons were not alarmed by what was taking place in Germany. Some sympathized with Germany because the country had suffered such a devastating defeat in World War I (1914–1918). British leaders did not want to think about invasion or war when memories of horrific World War I battles were still fresh in their minds. But increasingly, the public wanted to take a stand against German aggression.

A determined Churchill continued to expose the Hitler-Nazi threat. In turn, Hitler denounced Churchill, calling him a trouble-seeking warmonger. As Churchill and Hitler condemned each other throughout the 1930s, Hitler methodically carried out his plan to strengthen and increase what he considered a superior race and radically expand Germany's territories. He ordered boycotts of Jewish stores, burned books, and filled concentration camps with various minority groups and people who opposed his views. He trained young boys in military skills. He built factories that produced vast numbers of weapons and airplanes.

*Neville Chamberlain, left, and Adolf Hitler, right,
signed the Munich agreement on September 30, 1938.*

Despite his determination and best efforts,
Britain and the world continued to ignore
Churchill's warnings. They were convinced that
Churchill was wrong about Germany. They especially
hoped this after Neville Chamberlain, the British
prime minister, returned from a meeting with Hitler
in 1938 with a resolution—the Munich agreement—
signed by both leaders. It was a commitment to peace
in Europe—or so it was thought.

The Night of Broken Glass

Peace was merely wishful thinking. On October 15, 1938, Hitler sent German troops to occupy the Sudetenland—the western, northern, and southern borderlands of Czechoslovakia. This action broke the agreement he had signed with Chamberlain only two weeks earlier. On November 9, the Nazis carried out a 24-hour massive, brutal attack on Jews throughout Germany. They burned synagogues, wrecked Jewish homes and businesses, and beat and murdered Jewish men, women, and children.

Hitler: A Talented Speaker

Adolf Hitler's rise to power was due in part to his ability to move Germans with his powerful speeches. Many Germans responded to what he said, and how he said it, with awe. Crowds roared with approval as he shared his vision for Germany: jobs for everyone, a strong army, and restored pride. Beginning in a low voice, he urged his people on. As he spoke, Hitler's voice rose in excitement and volume. Carefully rehearsed hand gestures, facial expressions, and body movements, combined with emotion-packed words, brought audiences to a state of frenzy.

In a September 16, 1930, Nazi Party election speech, Hitler calmly began, "This election means that the circle is now complete. And the question at this time is: what are the aims of this opposition and its leaders?" By the end of his short speech, Hitler issued a call to arms: "Do not write on your banners the word 'Victory': today that word shall be uttered for the last time. Strike through the word 'Victory' and write . . . the word which suits us better— the word 'Fight.'"[3] Hitler's speeches rallied the Germans to action. His Nazi Party won control of the government in January 1933.

Approximately 25,000 Jewish men were sent to concentration camps. This event was called *Kristallnacht*—the night of broken glass.

The world began to lose its illusions about Hitler and Nazi Germany. Churchill became what some called a prophet of truth. On September 1, 1939, German forces invaded Poland. On September 3, Britain, Canada, France, Australia, and New Zealand declared war on Germany. World War II had begun.

GOVERNMENT APPOINTMENT

That same day, Chamberlain, the British prime minister, appointed Churchill first lord of the admiralty—head of the British navy—and gave Churchill a place on his war cabinet. Within days, the government sent the first British troops to France to protect Britain's allies from invasion.

The Nazi Party

The National Socialist German Workers Party, commonly known as the Nazi Party, was a political party in Germany from 1919 to 1945. Adolf Hitler became party leader in 1921.

Nazi principles included a belief in racial purity of the German people, known as Aryanism. Jews, even though they may have been born and raised in Germany, were considered enemies of the state and became unwelcome in their own country. The Nazis blamed the Jews for Germany's fall into poverty after World War I. The party also called for elimination of people the Nazis identified as enemies or unworthy of life. In addition to Jews, the mentally and physically disabled, socialists, communists, and homosexuals were also made outcasts. When Hitler's ideas of racial purity were put into practice, these beliefs resulted in the deaths of 6 million Jews and another 5 million non-Jews in what came to be known as the Holocaust.

The Parliament of the United Kingdom is the legislative body of Great Britain and British territories. Parliament's duties include passing laws, controlling taxation and the supply of money, declaring war, and making treaties. The symbolic head of government is the reigning monarch. The prime minister is normally the leader of the party that wins the election. He or she forms a governing cabinet from members of the party. Sometimes, as during World War II, the cabinet is a coalition, or group, of several parties. Parliament is divided into two houses: the House of Lords (upper house) and the House of Commons (lower house).

Seven months later, Britain lost its first major battle when German forces invaded Norway and Denmark even though the countries announced their neutrality and Hitler agreed to leave them alone. Then, on May 10, 1940, German forces invaded France, Belgium, Luxembourg, and the Netherlands. That evening, Chamberlain resigned as prime minister and recommended Churchill as his successor. King George VI, Britain's monarch, approved and appointed Churchill prime minister of Great Britain.

Churchill gave his first speech as prime minister on May 13, 1940. Standing before the House of Commons, he gave a powerful call to arms:

> *You ask, what is our policy? I can say: It is to wage war by sea, land and air, with all our might and with all the strength God can give us; to wage war against a monstrous tyranny, never surpassed*

in the dark, lamentable catalogue of human crime. That is our policy.

You ask, what is our aim? . . . It is victory, victory at all costs, victory in spite of all terror, victory, however long and hard the road may be; for without victory, there is no survival.[4]

As Churchill spoke, German forces pushed deeper into France. On June 3, 1940, they bombed Paris. On June 14, they took control of the capital city. Churchill was convinced that Britain would be next in Germany's westward path of aggression. Four days later, he again addressed the House of Commons:

I expect that the Battle of Britain is about to begin. Upon this battle depends the survival of Christian civilization. . . . Hitler knows that he will have to break us in this Island or lose the war. If we can stand up to him, all Europe may be free and the life of the world may move forward into broad, sunlit uplands. . . . Let us therefore brace ourselves to our duties, and so bear ourselves that if the British Empire and its Commonwealth last for a thousand years, men will still say, "This was their finest hour."[5]

The Swastika

The swastika—a stylized cross with arms bent at right angles—became the emblem of the Nazi Party and a sign of the Aryan race. Although the swastika had been used in the past for various religious and artistic purposes, its association with the Nazis makes it a controversial symbol today.

Churchill believed Britain would achieve ultimate victory. Although he was prepared for the challenges of World War II, Britain was not. He immediately set out to equip the country for war and to persuade a wavering, anxious people that victory was possible. Under Churchill's strong leadership, Britain would rally its greatest forces to pursue and defeat the most destructive powers of the time. Churchill would perform the momentous task he had expected most of his life. He would experience his finest hour as leader. ⌐

Nearly 100,000 Nazis gathered in Nuremberg, Germany,
on September 20, 1936, for the party's annual meeting.

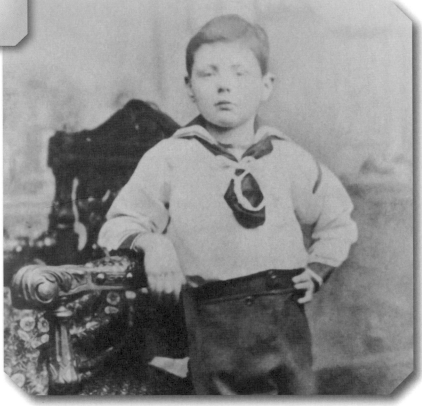

Winston Churchill at five years old

YOUNG WINSTON

ennie Jerome was the daughter of Leonard Jerome, a New York millionaire. When Jennie was 13 years old, her mother took Jennie and her two sisters to Europe for formal schooling and to advance their social lives. In August 1873, 19-year-old Jennie met Lord Randolph Churchill at a ball. He was a member of British nobility. Jennie and Lord Randolph were immediately attracted to one another and became engaged three days later. On April 15, 1874, the couple wed in a small ceremony at the British Embassy in Paris, France. Jennie Jerome was now Lady Randolph Churchill.

Winston Leonard Spencer Churchill was born at Blenheim Palace in Oxfordshire, England, on November 30, 1874. He was Lady and Lord Randolph Churchill's first child.

Woom

Winston was half American, but his upbringing was completely British. In the upper-class English tradition, Jennie did not care for her baby. Instead, a nanny, Elizabeth Anne Everest, took care of Winston's every need. Winston called her "Woom" or "Woomany," an early attempt to pronounce the word *woman*. The names stuck.

Blenheim Palace

John Churchill (1650–1722), an ancestor of Winston, fought important battles for Britain against King Louis XIV of France in the early eighteenth century. Parliament rewarded his victories by making him the first duke of Marlborough and building Blenheim Palace for him. When John Churchill died, his title and Blenheim Palace were inherited by the oldest son or daughter of the following generations. Since Winston's father was the third son of the seventh duke of Marlborough, he did not inherit the palace or the title of duke.

Jennie Jerome Churchill was born Jeanette Jerome on January 9, 1854, in Brooklyn, New York. She was one of three daughters. Her father was a wealthy businessman. Her mother was socially ambitious. Mrs. Jerome moved with her three daughters to Europe to provide the best opportunities to advance their social status.

Jennie did just that when she married Lord Randolph Churchill in 1874. As Lady Randolph, Jennie became a leader in London society. Five years after Lord Randolph's death in 1895, she married George Cornwallis-West, a good friend of Winston, considerably younger than she was. The couple divorced in 1914. Lady Randolph married Mantagu Porch, a soldier, in 1918.

In addition to being a socialite, wife, and mother, Lady Randolph was an author. She wrote her memoirs, *Reminiscences of Lady Randolph Churchill,* and the plays *Borrowed Plumes* and *The Bill.* Jennie Jerome Churchill died in 1921.

As a child, Winston rarely saw his parents. Winston's mother occasionally took him on a walk, read to him, or appeared for a goodnight kiss. At scheduled times, Woom brought a clean and well-dressed Winston to his parents for an "inspection" and progress report. Winston's parents often missed these appointments. Woom became Winston's main companion—his comforter, his strength, and his closest friend.

SCHOOLING BEGINS

In 1877, Winston's family and Woom moved to Ireland. Winston was happy there until Miss Hutchinson entered his life. He referred to her as "the Governess" and a "dreaded apparition."[1] She was a demanding tutor as she attempted to teach Winston reading and math. He understood the logic behind reading but hated math.

Woom worried about Winston. He always seemed to be ill with one cold after another. He also was plagued by a speech impediment and could not pronounce the letter *s*. Neither Winston's health nor his speech impediment prevented him from attending school.

St. George's School

In autumn 1880, Winston's brother John, known as Jack, was born. He would be Winston's only sibling. Later that year, the Churchill family returned to London. Two years later, Winston faced a challenge he dreaded more than the Governess: boarding school. In November 1882, he started attending St. George's School for boys. It offered an education that prepared students for various distinguished boarding schools, including his future alma mater, Harrow.

The day Winston arrived at St. George's, he was presented with his first lesson in Latin. He was told,

Churchill's American Ancestors

Most of Winston Churchill's American ancestors were colonists who arrived in America as early as 1650. At least four ancestors fought against the British in the American Revolutionary War. Samuel Jerome served in the militia of Berkshire County, Massachusetts. Major Libbeus Ball was with the Fourth Massachusetts Regiment and fought with George Washington at Valley Forge. Reuben Murray was a lieutenant in the regiments of Connecticut and New York. In addition, Lady Randolph's maternal great-grandmother was half Iroquois Indian.

"This is Latin grammar. You must learn this."[2]
The headmaster warned Winston that disrespect
would result in severe punishment: flogging with a
birch branch. The warning did not stop Winston
from questioning his education. He was repeatedly
beaten for his defiant behavior. Winston hated
the school. He did well in reading and history but
made little progress in subjects such as math, Latin,
and Greek. Winston loved to learn, but on his own
terms. In his opinion, these pointless lessons took
him away from all the interesting things he wanted
to do: romp in the garden or play in the nursery
with his toy soldiers. Winston had more than 1,000
lead soldiers, and the quantity grew each year. He
counted the days until he would return home to
the things he enjoyed, including lining up his toy
soldiers for battle on the nursery room floor.

Misses Thomson School

After spending two difficult years at St. George's,
Winston was transferred to the Misses Thomson
School, a small school in coastal Brighton. It was
run by two sisters, Kate and Charlotte Thomson.
Although Winston was much happier here than he
was at St. George's, he still ranked at the bottom

of his class for conduct. Through the kindness and understanding of the Thomson sisters, Winston began to improve.

Winston was allowed to study subjects that interested him. Before long, he was scoring at or near the top of his class in those subjects. He did especially well in English, French, and knowledge of the scriptures. His favorite classes were history, poetry, French, riding, and swimming. Winston began to enjoy school. In his free time, he read every newspaper he could find. He studied world events and followed the lives of political leaders.

Winston often wrote letters to his mother, and sometimes to his father, but he received

Lord Randolph Churchill

Lord Randolph Henry Spencer Churchill was born on February 13, 1849, in London, England. He was elected to the House of Commons in 1874, the year his son Winston was born.

Lord Randolph gave fiery speeches that verbally assaulted his opponents in Parliament. Despite his political enemies, Lord Randolph rose to the position of chancellor of the exchequer, the person in charge of Britain's finances. He also became leader of the House of Commons, an important parliamentary position. Lord Randolph was confident that he would soon become prime minister. However, in 1886, his political career essentially died when his proposed budget to drastically cut funds for the military was rejected by the cabinet; Lord Randolph resigned. He continued as a member of Parliament but lost his popularity and played no active government role. His health declined in the early 1890s. Lord Randolph died in 1895 at the age of 45.

A portrait of Lord Randolph Churchill, Winston Churchill's father

few replies. Winston invited his parents to visit him during the three years he was there, but they rarely came. Lord Randolph was in Brighton on business at least twice, but he did not visit his son. This did not surprise Winston. His father had always been too busy for him. Winston's parents did spend time with him when he came down with pneumonia at the age of 11. Both his mother and father stayed by his bedside until the crisis was over.

HARROW SCHOOL

When Winston returned home for holidays and school breaks, his parents often were traveling about Europe on social or political affairs. Winston spent most of his spare time with Woom, Jack, and his grandparents at Blenheim Palace. He was still fascinated with his collection of soldiers, which had grown to 1,500. He often lined them up for mock replays of historical battles he had read about.

When Winston turned 12, it was time for him to prepare for the examinations required to enter the elite Harrow School. He agonized over the many questions he was unable to answer. Despite his poor test scores, Winston was accepted into Harrow and placed in the lowest group. For daily roll call, the boys lined up according to academic rank. Winston uncomfortably took his place at the end of the line.

Winston's teachers were rarely pleased with his work, and his behavior was challenging for those around him. Assistant Master Henry Davidson

Language at Harrow

Because of his inability to grasp Latin and Greek, English was the only language Winston studied at Harrow. At the time, English was reserved for students who did not do well in school.

explained to Lady Randolph in a letter that Winston was not "in any way wilfully [sic] troublesome, but his forgetfulness, carelessness, unpunctuality, and irregularity in every way have really been so serious, that I write to ask you, when he is at home to speak gravely to him on the subject."[3]

Still, Winston received an award for reciting 1,200 lines from a famous poem from memory and won prizes in history. One teacher observed that Winston had "a brilliant brain, but he would only work when he chose to and for the matters he approved of."[4]

At the end of his days at Harrow, Winston would find where his unique mind and personality fit best: military school. He would discover that his endless energy and stubborn nature would one day make him an unbeatable leader who would intimidate some of Britain's greatest enemies.

Winston Churchill at 12 years old

Winston Churchill dressed as a Hussars officer, 1895

MILITARY TRAINING

In 1893, when Winston was 18, he was admitted to the Royal Military Academy at Sandhurst, an officer's training school. Winston attributed this decision to one day when his father visited Winston's collection of toy soldiers. Lord

Randolph studied the elaborate scene for 20 minutes. He was impressed by the troops that were in correct formation, ready for battle. At the end of his inspection, Lord Randolph asked his son if he would like to go into the army. Winston promptly responded that he did. He later wrote, "The toy soldiers turned the current of my life."[1]

SANDHURST

Sandhurst was a good fit for Winston. He studied subjects that interested him, including tactics, defense, mapmaking, military administration, and military law. He read books about war, artillery, infantry, and cavalry. He participated in building mock fortifications and blowing up bridges. Most of all, Winston enjoyed the riding school where soldiers trained for the cavalry. He was pleased when he qualified for the cavalry, but his father was not. The cavalry was very expensive since Winston had to pay for the care of his horse.

Sandhurst

The Royal Military Academy (RMA) was founded at Woolrich in 1741 and at Sandhurst in 1801. The Royal Military College (RMC) was founded in 1800. The RMA and the RMC closed in 1939 because of World War II. In 1947, the schools reopened as a single academic institution, the Royal Military Academy Sandhurst (RMAS). The school is still open today.

Two Great Losses

His disappointments aside, Lord Randolph seemed to respect his son more now that he was a gentleman cadet. For the first time in Winston's life, his father spent time with him. But their new friendship was short-lived. In spring 1894, Lord Randolph became critically ill. He died on January 24, 1895. All of Winston's dreams of comradeship, pleasing his father, and working beside him in Parliament were gone. Winston decided he must take his father's place, writing, "There remained for me only to pursue his aims and vindicate [remove blame from] his memory."[2] But Winston thought that if he was

---

Life at Sandhurst

Winston's enrollment at Sandhurst marked a new stage in his life. In an early letter to his father, Winston wrote about the school:

Of course it is very uncomfortable. No carpet or curtains. No ornamentation or adornments of any kind. No hot water and very little cold. . . . Hardly any law is given to juniors on joining. No excuse is ever taken . . . and of course no such thing as unpunctuality or untidiness is tolerated.[3]

This new experience was met with a new attitude. Winston's determination to succeed at Sandhurst is evident in the same letter when he wrote, "[There was] something very exhilarating in the military manner in which everything works; and I think that I shall like my life here during the next 18 months very much."[4]

In a letter from his tenth day at Sandhurst, Winston described his studies, writing, "The work is very interesting and extremely practical. Shot and shell of all kinds—bridges, guns, field and siege, mapping, keeping regimental savings bank accounts, inspecting meat etc."[5]

ever going to follow in his father's
political footsteps and be elected to
Parliament, he had to become famous
first. He believed the quickest path to
fame was to become a military hero.

Only months after his father died,
Winston suffered another loss. On
July 3, 1895, Woom died. Winston
had rushed to see her in London
when she became ill. He found a
good doctor to care for Woom, but
she slipped into unconsciousness.
Winston was at her bedside when she
died. He planned Woom's funeral,
paid for her headstone, and hired a
florist to maintain her grave.

Father and Son

Winston Churchill always
regretted that he and his
father did not have a close
relationship. He yearned
for his father's approval
yet never received it. He
later attributed his own
strength to this depriva-
tion, explaining, "Solitary
trees, if they grow at all,
grow strong; and a boy
deprived of a father's care
often developes [sic], if
he escapes the perils of
youth, an independence
and vigour of thought
which may restore in after
life the heavy loss of early
days."[6]

A Journey to Greatness Begins

Although 1895 was a sad year for Winston, it was
also one of achievements. Twenty-year-old Winston
finished eighth in his class of 150 at Sandhurst.
Shortly thereafter, a month after his father died,
Winston was conferred a military commission as
second lieutenant of the Fourth Hussars and joined
the cavalry. It was an honor to be a member of this

centuries-old British regiment with its rich history of battle honors. With his unhappy school years behind him, Winston entered a new and exciting world where he would begin his journey to greatness.

The next five years were busy and successful. He experienced combat on three continents, received four medals, wrote five books, was elected to Parliament, and became well known internationally. He recalled of this time, "All the days were good and each day better than the other."[7]

ADVENTURES IN CUBA

Cavalry life was expensive. Winston spent more on uniforms and the care of his horses than he was paid, but he was happy. Defending Britain was a huge task for the military. The British Empire ruled one-fourth of the world in the late 1890s. British citizens lived on every continent and on islands in every ocean. More than half of the 225,000 British troops were stationed outside England. A large segment of Britain's 17,000 cavalrymen were in India. Winston knew his regiment would be sent to India soon and took advantage of leave, or time off, he had coming. Instead of relaxing, he looked for adventure. He found it in Cuba, a colony of Spain.

Winston's mother set up the trip to the small island nation. She spoke with the British ambassador to Spain to obtain permission for her son to go to Cuba. When Winston arrived in Cuba in October 1895, the country was in the middle of a rebellion that Spanish troops were trying to crush. For 16 days, Winston experienced plenty of action as he traveled throughout Cuba with Spanish General Suarez Valdez. For three days, they were under fire on and off. Winston later wrote his mother that he had heard enough bullets whistle and hum past to satisfy him for some time to come.

Visiting Cuba

Winston Churchill's visit to Cuba in 1895 was not an unusual event at that time. Ambitious military officers often learned war tactics by seeing combat firsthand. There were numerous observers imbedded within the Spanish and U.S. armies in Cuba.

It was odd for Winston to be part of a foreign army. He was awarded Spain's Cross of the Order of Military Merit, but he was merely an observer. His role was to gather information for British intelligence and write reports on the conflict for the *Daily Graphic* newspaper. Winston's descriptive articles were popular, and he became known as a fine writer and journalist.

Winston's Love of Books

While he was stationed in India, Winston constantly asked his mother to send books. His favorites were about history. Winston begged his mother to send all 100 volumes of the *Annual Register*, a comprehensive guide to the history of the world, including long extracts from parliamentary debate. He asked also for the *Hansard*, the entire collection of parliamentary speeches. In addition, he read the Bible and works by Plato and Charles Darwin.

RETURN TO MILITARY LIFE

In autumn 1896, Winston returned to British military life. He was stationed for several years with the Fourth Hussars in India, which included what later became Pakistan. There were no immediate rebellions, so Winston played polo, read books, and wrote. He wrote his first and only novel, *Savrola: A Tale of the Revolution in Laurania.* Winston advised his friends not to read the book, and he never attempted another novel. However, he would continue to write nonfiction as a war correspondent.

Winston Churchill was stationed for several years with the Fourth Hussars in India.

As a young journalist, Winston Churchill worked as a correspondent for the Daily Graphic *and the* Morning Post.

SOLDIER, JOURNALIST, POLITICIAN

As much as Churchill enjoyed polo, reading, and writing, he was bored with military life in India. There was no action, and he was eager for adventure. In 1897, he heard about fighting along India's northwest border with

Afghanistan. He took a leave from his regiment and joined the expedition as a journalist. From his experiences there, Churchill wrote *The Story of the Malakand Field Force*. Published in 1898, the book became a great success.

Churchill's career as a war correspondent did not end in India. In 1898, there was an uprising in Sudan, Africa. A movement had been rebelling against British rule for seven years, and Britain was now fighting back. Churchill arrived in Sudan in September 1898 in the midst of the fierce Battle of Omdurman. He did more than report on the war, he fought in it. He rode his horse into masses of soldiers and killed those who raised their swords against him. The battle ended in a decisive British victory with thousands of enemy casualties.

The following year, Churchill resigned from the military. His military service was intended to be a stepping stone to politics, which had become his ultimate goal and greatest passion. He immediately ran for a seat in Parliament and lost. The common voter did not know enough about him yet.

Final Charge

When Churchill commanded a squadron of cavalry in the Battle of Omdurman in Sudan, Africa, in September 1898, it was the last cavalry charge in the history of warfare.

SOUTH AFRICA

After losing the election, Churchill had no
professional life. He became interested in a new
conflict raging in South Africa: the Boer War. Since
1886, numerous Englishmen had flocked to South
Africa's newly discovered gold and diamond mines.
The Boers—the Dutch residents—declared their
independence from Britain and denied the English
miners their civil rights. Churchill signed a contract
with London's *Morning Post* to be embedded with the
troops and report on the war.

In October 1899, Churchill set sail for Cape
Town, South Africa. Once there, he took a train
that stopped short of Ladysmith, where the Boers
had English troops under siege. The troops had only
three days of provisions. Churchill began writing. In
mid-November, he joined two companies traveling
by armored train to rescue the soldiers. Churchill
hired a special train to go as near as possible to
Ladysmith. The Boers ambushed and derailed
it. Churchill immediately took over, moving the
injured soldiers to cars that had not derailed.

The engine, which was harboring injured
soldiers, was able to get away. Churchill stayed
behind and faced armed Boers. He became a

prisoner of war. His enemies were delighted to capture the son of an English lord and took Churchill to their prison camp in Pretoria.

Being a prisoner left Churchill feeling frustrated, enraged, and hopeless. Within a few weeks, he escaped. The Boers searched for Churchill. "Wanted Dead or Alive" posters were hung throughout the region. Tired, hungry, and thirsty, Churchill knocked on the door of a house. A British miner greeted him. The miner hid Churchill until he could be smuggled onto a freight train. Churchill rode to Durban, where he was treated like a hero. Churchill was famous. Newspapers proclaimed his heroic feats. Telegrams praised his bravery.

Churchill stayed in Africa for six months more to report on and fight in the war. His reports were widely read. One of Churchill's greatest personal victories was freeing prisoners from the Pretoria camp where he had been held.

Churchill returned home in summer 1900. In October, he ran for a seat in Parliament and won. He was following in his father's footsteps.

Popular Speaker

Before he took his seat in Parliament, Churchill went on a speaking tour to earn money. Members of Parliament were not paid at that time, and Churchill needed to support his family. He gave 29 speeches in November 1900 alone—throughout Britain, the United States, and Canada.

In March 1901, Churchill took his seat in the House of Commons as a Conservative. In 1904, he switched to the Liberal Party. In 1905, he was named undersecretary of state for the colonies, his first ministerial post. In 1906, he won a landslide election and published a biography of his father. By 1908, he was president of the Board of Trade and one of the youngest senior cabinet ministers in Britain's history. Churchill was well on his way to becoming an influential politician. He would also soon become a husband and father.

Churchill Marries

Churchill first met Clementine Hozier in 1904. It was four years later, in March 1908, before they saw each other again. He did not make a good first impression on Hozier, but she was eventually won over by what she called his dominating charm and brilliance. They began exchanging letters and became more interested in each other. That summer, Churchill asked Hozier to marry him.

Lord Randolph's Biography

Churchill's two-volume biography of his father was published in 1906. He mainly wrote about Lord Randolph's political life and little about his personal life. Perhaps this was because Churchill had spent so little time with his father and barely knew him. Churchill based his facts largely on papers contained in his father's numerous tin boxes. He also referred to scrapbooks, newspaper articles, and letters written by other people.

Engagement photo of Clementine Hozier and Winston Churchill, 1908

On September 12, 1908, a cheering crowd of approximately 1,300 guests attended the couple's wedding in London. Their first child, Diana, was born on July 11, 1909. The couple would have four more children: Randolph, Sarah, Marigold, and Mary.

First Years as a Politician

Following his wedding and honeymoon, Churchill quickly got back to the business of politics. As president of the Board of Trade, he developed

Love Letters

Throughout their long life together, Winston and Clementine Churchill wrote letters to one another. The couple's exchanges were compiled into the book *Winston and Clementine: The Personal Letters of the Churchills* by daughter Mary. Published in 1998, the letters reveal Churchill's personal side, which was often sweet and romantic. One example is this undated letter to Clementine during their courtship:

My beloved – Get up! I want so much to see you. Let us go for a walk before lunch. . . . The sun shines bright, & my heart throbs to see you again – sweet – precious – Your devoted W.[1]

a program of social reform that included help for England's poor and working classes. He also created old-age pensions and unemployment insurance. Churchill devised what many called the "People's Budget," which would provide financial help to the needy.

In 1910, Churchill became home secretary. This position put him in charge of the police and prison system. He was genuinely concerned for prisoners—having been one himself—and supported prison reform. He also fought for better working conditions and improved safety for miners.

Churchill had many successes in his early government roles, but he also faced challenges. Suffragettes demonstrated because women were not allowed to vote at the time. It was Churchill's job to police these protests, which sometimes became extreme. Arrests were made, and Churchill had to deal with imprisoned women hunger strikers. Initially, he was not fully on the side of all suffragettes. Responding in anger, they disrupted his speeches and attacked him verbally. Eventually, he supported the right to vote for all women.

In addition to facing opposition from suffragettes, Churchill was strongly criticized for not sending soldiers to help police control a coal miners' strike that resulted in rioting and looting. Instead, he arranged a meeting between the strikers and mediators to find a solution. In another incident, he sent troops and a warship to subdue striking dock and railroad workers

The Churchill Children

Winston and Clementine Churchill had five children. Diana (1909–1963), worked as a Red Cross nurse during World War II and then joined the Women's Royal Naval Service. Her two marriages ended in divorce. Diana volunteered for the Samaritans, an organization that offered counseling to suicidal persons. Her own death in 1963 was ruled a suicide.

The Churchills' only son, Randolph (1911–1968), was a soldier and a writer. Randolph wrote the first two volumes of an eight-volume biography of his father.

The Churchills' second daughter, Sarah (1914–1982), worked in a photographic reconnaissance interpretation unit during World War II. She also became an accomplished actress. She is remembered for starring opposite Fred Astaire in the film *Royal Wedding* (1951).

Marigold (1918–1921), the Churchills' third daughter, died from meningitis as a toddler.

The youngest Churchill daughter, Mary, was born in 1922. She worked for the Red Cross between 1939 and 1941. She married a diplomat, Christopher Soames, who later became a politician. She is a successful writer. Her books include *Clementine Churchill*, a biography of her mother.

who were blocking food from entering the country. When rioters threw rocks at the troops, the soldiers shot and killed two people. Peace was restored by the end of the summer of 1911, but Churchill's status among the people had changed. Some praised him for taking control, some criticized his aggressive tactics, and others said he should have been tougher.

In October 1911, Churchill put the strikes and riots behind him when he was appointed first lord of the admiralty—head of the Royal Navy. He believed a strong navy had made Britain powerful and that a strong military was essential for survival. He put all his energy into this position. He visited naval bases and ships, improved sailors' conditions, and increased guns and supplies.

Churchill was aware of the growing tensions among several European nations. He especially kept watch on Germany and its massive buildup of military forces. Within a few years, Britain would be battling Germany, and the Royal Navy would be called upon to defend Britain at all costs. —

*First Lord of the Admiralty Winston Churchill
is dressed in his military uniform.*

The Great War, later known as World War I, divided Europe.

THE GREAT WAR

*U*nder Churchill's leadership, Britain's navy grew stronger. Germany's military power was growing as well. Churchill was troubled by Germany's skilled military strength and training practices. After visiting Germany and witnessing a massive military maneuver, Churchill was convinced the country was preparing for war. He warned fellow members of Parliament, but most believed France would provide a sufficient buffer zone between Great Britain and Germany. Churchill considered that wishful thinking and decided to prepare for war.

Churchill's main focus was the navy. British ships had to be better and faster than any others. Battleship guns had to be more powerful. Fascinated by aviation, which was less than a decade old, Churchill learned to fly before World War I and then established the Royal Naval Air Service to provide aerial protection for Britain's ships and ports.

THE GREAT WAR BEGINS

Tensions increased throughout the world. Countries such as France, Russia, Germany, the Ottoman Empire (present-day Turkey),

Royal Naval Air Service

Britain's naval aviation branch was called the Royal Naval Air Service (RNAS) until nearly the end of World War I. It had 12 air stations along the coast of Britain and boasted seaplanes, carrier aircraft, and fighter squadrons. The RNAS patrolled England's vast coast along the English Channel and the North Sea to watch for enemy vessels. RNAS pilots sometimes provided aerial protection over London. At times, airplanes were deployed to Germany for air raids on German air stations. RNAS pilots used seaplanes when missions took them over the Atlantic Ocean. The RNAS also fought on land, using armored cars manufactured by Rolls-Royce.

In 1918, the RNAS merged with the British army's Royal Flying Corps and created a new military branch: the Royal Air Force (RAF). The RNAS contributed 67,000 military personnel, nearly 3,000 aircraft, 103 airships, and 126 stations on Britain's coast. After World War I, the RAF was cut drastically.

Belgium, and Austria-Hungary were involved in political conflicts. On June 28, 1914, Franz Ferdinand, heir to the Austro-Hungarian Empire, was assassinated. The event sparked the Great War, which later became known as World War I. Major European powers were quickly pulled into the fighting.

On August 1, 1914, Germany declared war on Russia. Germany declared war on France on August 3 and invaded neutral Belgium the following day. Late on August 4, Churchill ordered all British ships and naval bases, "Commence hostilities against Germany."[1]

The navy guarded Britain's

Letter to Clementine

On July 31, 1914, Churchill wrote to his wife, Clementine, about the declining political relations in Europe.

My darling –

There is still hope although the clouds are black & blacker. Germany is realizing I think how great are the forces against her, & is trying tardily to restrain her idiot ally. We are working to soothe Russia. But everybody is preparing swiftly for war and at any moment now the stroke may fall. We are ready.

Churchill's focus was on home as well as on international affairs. He went on to discuss personal financial matters, writing:

I am perturbed at the expense for this month . . . I will pay the bills direct myself. . . . I am sending you the cheque for Pear Tree. I am so glad you find rest and contentment there.

Fondest love my darling one –
Your devoted husband
W[2]

bridges, searched all boats, and set up a watch along Britain's coastlines. British sailors numbering 120,000 were positioned on ships in the English Channel. Part of the naval fleet was moved to the North Sea to take up battle stations.

Churchill was convinced that Great Britain was at risk. In speech after speech, he rallied Britons to fight and inspired national pride. But his popularity faded when three British ships were torpedoed and sunk in the first few weeks of the war. The public blamed him for the 1,459 casualties aboard those ships. Newspapers referred to the casualties as "Winston's war babies." But the public praised him two months later when Britain won a naval victory in the south Atlantic.

Great War Alliances

There were two alliances during the Great War. The Allied Powers included Great Britain, France, Russia, Belgium, Serbia, Montenegro, Japan, Italy, and the United States. The Central Powers were Austria-Hungary, Bulgaria, Germany, and the Ottoman Empire. The war ultimately involved more than two dozen countries, though not all of them were actually involved in conflict.

FIGHTING ON LAND

In preparation for war, Churchill established the Royal Navy Division (RND) with volunteers trained to fight on land. For their protection, he suggested building landships. These armored vehicles with caterpillar tracks and built-in machine guns, called tanks, were designed to crush everything in their paths. Churchill convinced Herbert Asquith, the British prime minister, to go along with his idea, and the Landships Committee of the Admiralty was formed.

In late 1914, German troops surrounded Antwerp, Belgium, a portal to the North Sea. Churchill visited the city. Within days, he sent 8,000 RND soldiers to fight German forces. The tiny Belgian army and the RND were unable to stand up against 60,000 German troops. After five days of fighting with 20,000 Belgian casualties, 1,500 British troops taken prisoner, and nearly 1,000 more missing, the city surrendered.

The public criticized Churchill. Disheartened by his military failure in Antwerp, he fell into depression and considered resigning. But at the end of 1914, he had a new position: member of the War Council. This group set British war policies.

THE DARDANELLES

At the beginning of 1915, Churchill was again actively involved in the war. British troops fought vicious battles from muddy trenches as they tried to prevent Germany's westward drive. Opposing armies were in a standoff, but Churchill took action. His first plan was to take control of the Dardanelles, a narrow strait through northwestern Ottoman Empire. Victory would make it possible for Britain to capture Constantinople (present-day Istanbul), the capital of the Ottoman Empire. Technically, the Ottoman Empire was a neutral country, but it was leaning toward supporting Germany in the war. By opening up the passageway, Britain's ally, Russia, would weaken the Ottoman Empire and strengthen the Allies.

The Dardanelles

A narrow strait through northwestern Turkey, the Dardanelles is an important water passageway. It connects the Aegean Sea and the Sea of Marmara, linking with the Black Sea and Russia. This international waterway separates Europe from mainland Asia. The Dardanelles has been a coveted waterway in numerous naval battles throughout history.

On March 18, 1915, British and French battleships arrived off the coast of the Ottoman Empire. Several ships hit underwater mines and sank. Turkish machine guns on the cliffs above the Dardanelles posed another threat. In April, an Allied land invasion of the Gallipoli peninsula in the Ottoman Empire proved disastrous. Several thousand troops were killed. Once again, the public harshly criticized Churchill. Asquith, the British prime minister, fired him as first lord of

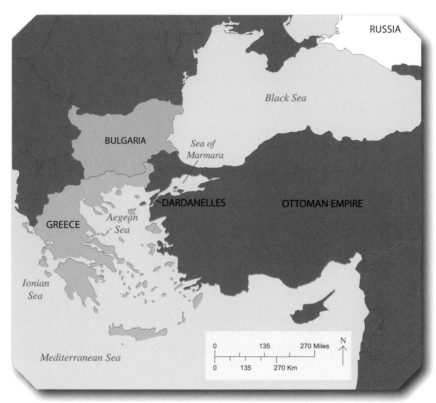

*The Dardanelles became an important battleground
for Britain and the Allies during World War I.*

the admiralty and offered him a position with little
responsibility: chancellor of the Duchy of Lancaster.
Churchill reluctantly accepted. Although he still
retained his seat on the War Council, he had little
power to make decisions.

Churchill fell into the deepest depression
of his life. Clementine later told her husband's

biographer, Martin Gilbert, "I thought he would never get over the Dardanelles; I thought he would die of grief."[3] Churchill tried to divert his attention from the war by vacationing, exercising, socializing, and golfing. These distractions did little to help him. Churchill's sister-in-law suggested he try painting. He painted still lifes and landscapes of Britain's countryside. Churchill enjoyed it and did well. Painting was good therapy for him.

Churchill also spent time with his children and two nephews. He played with them for hours, but his mind was still on the war. He constantly followed its progress, but was powerless to make decisions.

A Soldier Again

After nearly six months of idleness, Churchill found a way to become involved again in the war. He signed up to command the Royal Scots Fusiliers in the trenches of Flanders, Belgium. Churchill had escaped death in the Boer War and other battles. He now skirted death while others around him were falling. He was convinced that he was protected by a higher power for a greater task.

Churchill continued to write while he led his troops. He was asked to give an opinion on a new

Churchill's love of painting with oils began during World War I and continued throughout his life. Churchill painted this picture in 1929.

offensive under consideration for the Dardanelles. In his paper "Variants of the Offensive," he promoted the use of body armor, tanks, and surprise attacks. In May 1916, Churchill returned to London, barging into Parliament and demanding the removal of several admirals. He criticized the War Office and suggested new weapons and surprise tactics. Churchill's outspoken manner made him increasingly unpopular, but he did not care. He wanted to win the war. Allied troops were being massacred, and no relief from the brutal battles was in sight.

A New Role

Asquith resigned as British prime minister in
December 1916. David Lloyd George succeeded
him. Lloyd George admired Churchill. In March
1917, Lloyd George cleared him of any blame for
the Dardanelles disaster. In July, Lloyd George
appointed Churchill minister of munitions, in
charge of war supplies.

The war was not going well for Britain and
the Allies. German U-boats, or submarines, had
destroyed British ships and several passenger liners.
Germany bombed cities and used poisonous mustard
gas. Russia could not provide much help to the Allies
because it was fighting an internal revolution. The
United States was now involved in the war, but U.S.
troops would not be prepared to fight alongside the
Allies until 1918.

Victory

By autumn 1918, Churchill's landship, the tank,
turned the tide of war. The armored vehicles helped
batter and defeat German forces. The Allies also
made full use of airplanes and poisonous mustard
gas to bring down the enemy. With Churchill's
strategic war tactics and the addition of U.S. troops,

victory was in sight. Austria-Hungary was the first to surrender, followed by Germany. An armistice was signed on November 11, 1918, silencing the battlefields.

In December 1918, Lloyd George appointed Churchill secretary of state for war and air. On June 28, 1919, the Treaty of Versailles officially ended the war. Part of Churchill's job was to impose reparations, or payment for damages done during the war, on Germany. Churchill suggested sending food to the war-ravaged country, but Lloyd George would not allow it. The public cried out for punishment.

British citizens celebrated their victory and called it the last great war in the history of the world. Churchill was not so optimistic. He foresaw another war in Europe and ordered all leftover weapons put into storage. Meanwhile, Germany's people would soon welcome a leader who would promise them not only status, but revenge: Adolf Hitler.

"For four years Germany fought and defied the five continents of the world by land and sea and air. . . . To break their strength and science and curb their fury, it was necessary to bring all the greatest nations of mankind into the field against them. . . . Small states were trampled down in the struggle; a mighty Empire was battered into unrecognizable fragments; and nearly twenty million men perished or shed their blood before the sword was wrested from that terrible hand. Surely, Germans, for history it is enough!"[4]

—Winston Churchill

German Chancellor Adolf Hitler would become Winston Churchill's adversary.

Winston Churchill at home in 1929

WILDERNESS YEARS

*I*t would be 21 years before Britain would
again be at war. During that time,
Churchill's life was uneventful compared to the war
years. In January 1921, he was appointed secretary
of state for the colonies. Put in charge of Britain's

colonies, Churchill kept his eye on India and Ireland, which were moving toward independence.

MANY LOSSES

Although 1921 brought Churchill success with a new government position, the Churchill family faced multiple tragedies that year. Clementine's brother and Churchill's mother died. Churchill was at his mother's bedside when she died. Although she had married twice since Lord Randolph died, she was buried next to him. Then another tragedy struck: Churchill's youngest child, two-year-old Marigold, died of meningitis. After her death, Churchill went to Scotland alone. There, he found comfort painting.

Churchill's losses and difficult times continued for two more years. In October 1922, he lost his seat in the cabinet. In November, he also lost the election for the House of Commons. It was the first time in 22 years Churchill did not hold a seat in Parliament. He lost the election again in 1923.

Churchill's Love of Painting

Churchill enjoyed painting for more than 40 years. Few knew he was a talented painter until 1948, when his 1921 essay "Painting as a Pastime" was published in book form. Churchill did not draw attention to his paintings and avoided public displays of his art. He was afraid people would like his art for who he was rather than for how he painted. His works were first exhibited in France under the assumed name of Charles Morin.

New Possibilities

The year 1924 brought new possibilities to Churchill. He returned to the Conservative Party and won the election. The new prime minister, Stanley Baldwin, appointed Churchill chancellor of the exchequer, the same position his father had once held. When accepting the position, he said, "This fulfils [sic] my ambition. I still have my father's robe as Chancellor. I shall be proud to serve you in this splendid Office."[1] Presenting yearly budgets and handling Britain's money was quite an unusual position for someone who hated math and saw no logic in numbers. Churchill put all his energy into the position. He used his position to help expand social reforms, which included granting pensions to widows and orphans.

Churchill's new role was not without challenges. Prices of British exports increased, which made other countries reduce their trading with Britain. This weakened the British economy, for which Churchill was criticized. Coal miners went on strike in 1926, setting off a nine-day general strike in all of Britain's industries. Churchill's negotiating skills and sense of fairness helped end both the general strike and the coal strike.

CHARTWELL

In 1927 and 1928, Churchill spent many weekends at Chartwell. He had purchased this second home in the countryside near London for his family in 1922. Although he isolated himself in his study to manage political affairs, Churchill enjoyed the rest of the estate with his children. In the dining room, he played charades and acted in plays. In the garden, he built a tree house for his older children. For his youngest child, he built a little brick house.

Churchill hosted many affairs at Chartwell, but he mainly focused on his family and many animals there.

Chartwell

Churchill bought Chartwell in 1922. He lived there with his family for 40 years. He was fascinated with its location in a shallow valley with Crockham Hill to the west and Toys Hill to the east. The valley had a lake fed by the Chart Well.

When Churchill was not serving in Parliament or fighting a war, his daily routine at Chartwell was relaxed. Awake by 7:30 a.m., he breakfasted in bed with his mail and newspapers. For the next few hours, he dictated from his bed to his secretaries. At about 11:00 a.m., he got up, bathed, and walked outside or worked in his study. A three-course lunch was served at 1:30 p.m. for his family and any guests. At about 3:30 p.m., he returned to his study, managed Chartwell's affairs, or played backgammon or cards with his wife. At 5:00 p.m., he napped for 90 minutes. At 6:30 p.m., he bathed again and dressed for the 8:30 p.m. dinner, which was the highlight of his day. The meal and lively conversations often lasted until about 10:30, but Churchill's day still was not finished. He often worked until 3:00 a.m. before turning in for the night.

Chartwell, Winston Churchill's country estate

KEEPING BUSY

Churchill often gave speeches during this time. In his yearly budget speeches in Parliament, he also discussed issues unrelated to the country's finances, such as the threat of socialism and communism. Because of his positions, he was considered by many to be a warmonger. In the 1929 election, the Conservative Party was defeated. Churchill's term as exchequer ended. It was not a highly successful term, but he had dutifully performed his job and dealt wisely with opposition.

In 1930, Churchill finished writing his autobiography, *My Early Life*. The international best seller brought in enough money to support his family through the hard times that would come in the 1930s.

As a member of Parliament, Churchill remained actively involved in Britain's political affairs. Throughout 1931, he vigorously debated against Britain granting independence to India. As a result, he was not given a place in Britain's national government.

With no major political responsibilities or influence, Churchill spoke frequently in Parliament. He also received visitors from every aspect of British life who provided information that enabled him to remain at the center of knowledge and debate. He spent much of his time writing books. Churchill referred to this period of his life as his wilderness years.

In December 1931, Churchill traveled to New York City. During his visit, he was struck by a car. While recovering from his injuries, an infection kept him hospitalized for eight days. Again, he was convinced

Prolific Writer

In his lifetime, Churchill wrote 71 books—including his four-volume *History of the English-Speaking Peoples*—and numerous papers and articles.

that his life had been spared so he could fulfill some great destiny.

INTEREST IN GERMANY

On a trip to Munich in 1932, Churchill happened to meet one of Hitler's associates, who encouraged him to meet Hitler. A meeting of the two men was arranged, but then cancelled after Churchill asked:

> Why is your chief so violent about the Jews? . . . [W]hat is the sense of being against a man simply because of his birth? How can any man help how he is born?[2]

That year, the Nazi Party became Germany's leading political party. After an election in January 1933, party leader Adolf Hitler became Germany's leader. He proceeded to establish absolute power and form a regime known as the Third Reich. Germany now had a dictator. Hitler's military guard was the *Schutzstaffel*, or SS for short. The SS immediately began gathering dissidents, or critics of the regime, and taking them to concentration camps to be beaten, tortured, and often killed.

Churchill was worried about Hitler and Germany, but his warnings to Parliament and the public went unheeded. Most Britons mistrusted him. Many claimed that he misunderstood the Germans. Churchill wrote about Parliament's response to his warnings, "I felt a sensation of despair."[3]

Some Parliament members would not listen to Churchill at all and left whenever he rose to speak. Opposition did not deter Churchill. He unceasingly told his country to watch Germany, make more war materials, and prepare its military for a possible invasion.

GERMAN EXPANSION

In 1936, Germany welcomed the world to Berlin for the summer Olympics. Many people were glad to see Germany's dignity and well-being restored after the devastation of World War I. That same year, the Nazis marched unopposed into the Rhineland in western Germany and occupied the region.

Nazi Beliefs and Practices

Nazi ideology emphasized the purity of the Aryan race, which meant fair-skinned, blond northern Europeans. Anyone who did not fit this description was viewed as an enemy of the Nazi Party and not worthy of living freely.

Nazis specifically targeted Jews, gypsies, Jehovah's Witnesses, Socialists, Communists, homosexuals, and the physically and mentally disabled. Extermination of these people, especially Jews, took place in numerous concentration camps throughout Europe. People were either shot or put in gas chambers to die. Huge crematoriums at the camps burned millions of dead bodies by the end of the war in 1945. Approximately 11 million people died in concentration camps during World War II, and more than 40 million died in the fighting.

In early 1938, the Nazis took control of Austria. Hitler wanted the Sudetenland next, the part of Czechoslovakia where people of German descent lived. On September 30, 1938, Neville Chamberlain, the British prime minister, met with Hitler. The two men signed the Munich agreement, which allowed Germany to occupy the area. Chamberlain was convinced that the Sudetenland was all Hitler wanted. He believed that appeasing Hitler would bring peace. Chamberlain returned to Britain, waved the agreement in the air, and victoriously declared peace. People worldwide praised Chamberlain for avoiding a war.

With foreboding, Churchill declared, "We have sustained a defeat without a war. . . . And do not suppose that this is the end. . . . This is only the first sip, the first foretaste of a bitter cup."[4] That bitter cup would be World War II, and Churchill's importance as leader would soon be recognized.

Adolf Hitler addresses a crowd of 80,000 workers
in Berlin, Germany, on May 1, 1936.

Winston Churchill prepares to fly.

WORLD WAR II

In March 1939, German troops took control of Czechoslovakia. Chamberlain and members of Parliament finally heeded Churchill's warnings about Hitler. A ministry of supply was established to oversee the manufacturing of British war materials. Many members of the public were disappointed that this ministry was not given to Churchill. Newspaper editorials called for Churchill to be given a cabinet position. Churchill waited in vain for a telephone call that would invite him to join the war cabinet.

On September 1, 1939, German forces invaded Poland—the first of Germany's blitzkrieg ("lightning war") campaigns. Britain, Canada, France, Australia, and New Zealand declared war on Germany two days later. More than 2,000 German tanks and 1,000 airplanes encircled Warsaw, the capital of Poland. Britain demanded that Germany withdraw from Poland, but Hitler ignored the demand. Warsaw surrendered to Germany on September 27.

On the day Britain declared war on Germany, Churchill received an appointment to the war cabinet. He was also appointed first lord of the admiralty—the position he had held from 1911 to 1915.

Blitzkrieg

Germany's blitzkrieg was a strategy based on speed and surprise. The military surge used a combination of infantry (foot soldiers), light tanks, and aircraft to attack swiftly before the opposition had a chance to mobilize resistance. In the first years of World War II, this method of fighting had a disastrous effect on British and French armies. They were defeated in a matter of a few weeks. This type of warfare was different from the stationary warfare fought from the trenches of World War I. Blitzkrieg was designed to move fast, hit hard, and create a panic among civilians and military troops.

CHURCHILL BECOMES PRIME MINISTER

Chamberlain planned to remain prime minister until the end of the battle in France. But he was not up to leading Britain during the war, and he did not have the full support of Parliament. A united government of all parties was desirable during the war, but Labour Party members were clear that they would not serve under him. On May 10, 1940, Chamberlain stepped down as prime minister and recommended Churchill to succeed him. King George VI approved, and 65-year-old Winston Churchill was appointed prime minister of Great Britain. Churchill was relieved that the great task he had been waiting for all his life had finally arrived. He later explained his experience of that night, writing, "I felt as if I were walking with destiny, and that all my past life had been but a preparation for this hour and for this trial."[1]

On the day Churchill was appointed prime minister, Hitler's army and air force unleashed its

Churchill on Napping

Winston Churchill became prime minister at an age when many people retire. He said he was able to keep up his daily pace and cope because he took an afternoon nap. On the subject of naps, he wrote, "Nature had not intended mankind to work from eight in the morning until midnight without that refreshment of blessed oblivion which, even if it only lasts twenty minutes, is sufficient to renew all the vital forces."[2]

blitzkrieg on Belgium, France, and the Netherlands. Three days later, Churchill gave his first speech as prime minister to the House of Commons. He ended with a call to arms: "I say, 'come, then, let us go forward together with our united strength.'"[3] The British people finally had hope in a strong leader.

Churchill visited naval bases, inspected new battleships, and sent troops to France. He ordered freighters and passenger ships to return to British or neutral ports. He worked tirelessly.

House of Commons

I beg to move,

That this House welcomes the formation of a Government representing the united and inflexible resolve of the nation to prosecute the war with Germany to a victorious conclusion. . . . [W]e are in the preliminary stage of one of the greatest battles in history . . . many preparations . . . have to be made here at home. . . . I would say to the House, . . . "I have nothing to offer but blood, toil, tears and sweat."

We have before us an ordeal of the most grievous kind. . . . many long months of struggle and of suffering. You ask, what is our policy? . . . It is to wage war, by sea, land and air, with all our might . . . against a monstrous tyranny. . . . You ask, what is our aim? . . . It is victory . . . at all costs . . . in spite of all terror . . . however long and hard the road may be; for without victory, there is no survival. . . . for the British Empire . . . for all that the British Empire has stood for . . . But I take up my task with . . . hope. . . . At this time . . . I say, "come then, let us go forward together with our united strength."[4]

—Winston Churchill
First Speech as Prime Minister
May 13, 1940

Winston Churchill watches a Stirling bomber taxi across an airfield.

President Roosevelt

A week after Churchill was appointed prime minister, he contacted U.S. President Franklin Roosevelt for help. The two statesmen had corresponded regularly since 1939, when Roosevelt had expressed how glad he was that Churchill was again lord of the admiralty. But as much as Roosevelt wanted to help Britain, the U.S. Congress firmly refused to intervene in a war it said was Europe's problem.

Britain Struggles

The war had not gone well for Britain and the Allies. In September 1939, the Royal Navy lost the aircraft carrier *Courageous*. The Germans sank the battleship *Royal Oak* in October. In April 1940, Britain lost a major battle when Germany invaded Denmark and Norway. In May, German forces invaded France, Belgium, Luxembourg, and the Netherlands. The British and French evacuated approximately 335,000 soldiers on nearly 1,000 sea vessels, of which 243 were sunk. The next day, the Germans bombed Paris.

Even as Germany invaded France, some British cabinet members still encouraged Churchill to negotiate with Germany. He refused. Churchill addressed the House of Commons on June 4, 1940:

> *We shall go on to the end. We shall fight in France, we shall fight in the seas and oceans, we shall fight with growing confidence and growing strengths in the air, we shall defend our island, whatever the cost may be.*[5]

House members cheered and applauded. Many had tears in their eyes.

Considerable Correspondence

During World War II, Churchill wrote to Roosevelt 950 times and received approximately 800 responses.

World War II Alliances

There were two alliances during World War II. The Allied Powers included Great Britain, the United States, and the Soviet Union. The major Axis Powers were Germany, Italy, and Japan.

Six days later, Germany's ally Italy declared war on Britain and France. On June 14, 1940, German troops marched into and occupied Paris, the capital of France. Germany and Italy then quickly swept through France in a defeat swifter than any seen before. From the northern French port city of Calais, the Germans now had a clear view of Dover, England, which was located directly across the narrowest part of the English Channel. As Germany kept watch on England's shores, U-boats continued to attack battleships and merchant ships in the Atlantic Ocean.

The war during Churchill's first six weeks as prime minister saw the defeat of the Netherlands, Belgium, and France. Once the battle of France was lost, Britain was virtually left alone to fight the Germans and their allies, as well as defend the vulnerable shores of England. ⌐

Allies

Axis

Axis Controlled

Neutral Nations

0   621 miles (1,000 km)

N

Atlantic Ocean

Sweden

Norway

Finland

Soviet Union

Denmark

Latvia

Lithuania

East Prussia

The Netherlands

Ireland

Great Britain

Poland

Belgium

Greater Germany

Luxembourg

Czechoslovakia

France

Switzerland

Hungary

Austria

Romania

Yugoslavia

Italy

Bulgaria

Black Sea

Albania

Portugal

Spain

Greece

Turkey

Spanish Morocco

Tunisia

Cyprus

Syria

Mediterranean Sea

Palestine

Morocco

Algeria

Libya

Egypt

The division of Europe in 1945 as a result of World War II

*Winston Churchill visits the bombed city
of Bristol, England, in April 1941.*

The Battle of Britain

Through late July and early August 1940, the Battle of Britain raged on. Germans bombed British airfields and aircraft factories. On August 23, the Germans began bombing London. Britain retaliated with air raids over Berlin.

In September, Hitler implemented an all-out blitz against Britain in preparation for invasion. Germany's strategy was to attack at night by air. Two hundred German bombers attacked London on September 7, 1940. The next day, Churchill traveled the streets of the city, talking to survivors. At one stop, some shouted, "We thought you'd come. We can take it. Give it 'em back."[1] Churchill's constant encouragement was his victory sign—his first and second fingers held high in the shape of a *V*.

United and Undaunted

Churchill regularly visited bomb-damaged cities and talked with residents whose homes had been destroyed or family members killed. Churchill was moved to tears by the bravery he saw in the common people. He regularly watched the bombardment from the roof of 10 Downing Street, the official London residence of the prime minister. Although he had an armored car, Churchill refused to use it on his trips to bomb-damaged cities.

"Far be it from me to paint a rosy picture of the future. Indeed, I do not think we should be justified in using any but the most sombre tones and colours while our people, our Empire and indeed the whole English-speaking world are passing through a dark and deadly valley. But I should be failing in my duty if, on the other wise, I were not to convey the true impression, that a great nation is getting into its war stride."[2]

—*Winston Churchill*
January 22, 1941
House of Commons

Britain's resources were dwindling. Massive air raids continued to pummel British cities. British children were evacuated to the countryside to escape danger and devastation in the cities. The determination of the British people was weakening. Churchill spoke honestly in a radio address:

> Long, dark nights of trials and tribulations lie before us. . . . Death and sorrow will be companions of our journey, constancy and valor our only shield. We must be united, we must be undaunted. We must be inflexible.[3]

Britain's enemies—the Axis powers—grew with the addition of Hungary, Bulgaria, and Romania. These powers invaded Greece, Egypt, and Yugoslavia. British troops hurried to Greece and Egypt to help defend those nations.

By November 1940, British air defense prevented the possibility of invasion. However, the Germans continued their massive air raid on British cities. The bombing continued into spring 1941. Within eight months, more than 60,000 British citizens were killed, and the centers of many of England's major cities were destroyed.

The Battle of the Atlantic was continuous throughout the early 1940s. During this battle, the

Allies worked to keep the waters free of U-boats. The Germans wanted to keep the British from receiving troops and supplies from across the Atlantic. If German ships managed to block the waters, Britain would starve and be forced to surrender.

On June 22, 1941, Churchill awoke to news that Germany had attacked the Soviet Union. Churchill strongly opposed the Soviet Union's Communist system. But he agreed to work with Soviet leader Joseph Stalin in order to fight Germany, their now mutual enemy. Churchill supplied Stalin with every war material: tanks, aircraft, ships, militia, and secret intelligence. Churchill persuaded Roosevelt to do the same.

Churchill's Offices during the War

In the 1920s and 1930s, Britain feared that one day the country's cities, especially London, might be the target of enemy bombs. The country built bunkers beneath London to provide a safe place for the government to continue operating if that occurred.

One set of bunkers was the Cabinet War Rooms. It included a large room where government officials met during German air raids. Churchill's offices were above ground, immediately above the Cabinet War Rooms. He would return to 10 Downing Street to meet military leaders. He lunched regularly with King George VI at 10 Downing Street. On four occasions during the war, Churchill gave radio broadcasts to the world from the underground Cabinet War Rooms. The rest of his broadcasts were made from the British Broadcasting Corporation. From the Transatlantic Telephone Room, Churchill communicated on a scrambled telephone line with President Roosevelt to make plans in complete secrecy.

U-110

During World War II, British and U.S. navies damaged several U-boats. Allied forces gained valuable information from these submarines. In 1941, British sailors forced the crew of the German U-boat *U-110* to abandon the submarine. British servicemen boarded *U-110* and discovered the sophisticated German coding and cipher system, the Enigma machine, and its cipher keys, keybooks, and other important cryptographic records. These valuable pieces of Germany's secret intelligence system eventually played a large part in an Allied victory in the Atlantic. *U-110* was towed behind a British ship and allowed to sink "accidentally" approximately 100 miles (160 km) from Iceland. This was done so that the Germans would not become suspicious and change all the cipher codes before the Allies could use them.

THE ATLANTIC CONFERENCE

On August 9, 1941, Churchill and Roosevelt met off the coast of Newfoundland on the *Augusta*. The secret meeting—the Atlantic Conference—was the first time the two men met face-to-face. For the next three days, the two leaders tackled the major issues of the war. Although the United States was still not part of the war, Roosevelt discussed with Churchill how to help Britain against Hitler and Italian leader Benito Mussolini.

By the end of the conference, Churchill and Roosevelt devised the Atlantic Charter. It was a vision of democracy and freedom for a post-World War II world. They also formed a "Grand Alliance" against the Axis powers, although Churchill remained disappointed that the United States had still not entered the war.

U.S. Involvement in the War

On December 7, 1941, just four months after the historic summit, Japan bombed Pearl Harbor, Hawaii. On December 8, the United States declared war on Japan and officially entered World War II. Britain also declared war on Japan that day. On December 11, Germany and Italy declared war on the United States. By the end of January 1942, the first U.S. troops arrived abroad.

Churchill and Roosevelt continued to meet throughout the war to discuss tactics. They made plans for their troops to cross the English Channel in a huge assault on German-occupied France. They would defeat Germany first and then target Japan. Meanwhile, Churchill traveled to countries damaged by the war. He also visited Stalin in Moscow.

Turning Point

In November 1942, an Allied victory in Egypt proved to be a turning point of the war. Churchill announced to a British audience:

> *We have a new experience. We have victory—a remarkable and definite victory. Now this is not the end. It is not even the beginning of the end. But it is, perhaps, the end of the beginning.* [4]

Churchill's health was not good in 1943. He
suffered from pneumonia and three mild heart
attacks that year. His physical problems were hidden
from the public to sustain morale. In spite of his
ailments, Churchill maintained a close watch on
the conduct of the war. On July 28, 1943, the
RAF killed more than 42,000 civilians during a
43-minute bombing raid on Hamburg, Germany.
From November 28 through December 1, Churchill
met with Roosevelt and Stalin for the first time. The
three major Allied leaders met in Tehran, Iran, to
discuss the war and plan a strategy to defeat Germany
and its allies.

By spring 1944, Allied leaders completed plans
for Operation Overlord—the liberation of France.

**The RAF during
World War II**

The Royal Air Force (RAF)
was drastically cut after
World War I. As World
War II intensified, the RAF
became Britain's main
defense against the Luft-
waffe, Germany's power-
ful air force. In addition
to protecting Britain, the
RAF carried out numer-
ous bombing campaigns
against Germany.

On June 6, 1944, more than
150,000 Allied soldiers arrived by
air and sea to land on the beaches of
Normandy, France. Despite heavy
casualties from German machine-
gun fire, the Allies were victorious.
By the end of August, the French
coastline was liberated. Allied troops
moved eastward and entered Paris.
The Germans retreated.

By 1944, the German armies were driven back in both western and eastern Europe. Churchill, Roosevelt, and Stalin met a second time, at Yalta, Russia, to discuss Japan and postwar Europe. Two months later, the Allies liberated prisoners from concentration camps in Germany. Roosevelt died on the day the Buchenwald camp was liberated, April 12, 1945. Roosevelt's death was a huge blow to Churchill. He lost a personal and political ally. Nine days after Roosevelt's death, Soviet troops entered Berlin. On April 30, 1945, Hitler committed suicide inside his underground Berlin bunker. On May 7, all German forces surrendered. The next day, the Allies celebrated—it was called V-E (Victory in Europe) Day.

Jubilant Britons lined the streets to cheer Churchill. Members of his staff applauded as he walked to Parliament. In the House of Commons, the shouts were deafening when he entered. Churchill thanked everyone, and then followed the

Nazi Gas Chambers

During World War II, the Nazis used gas chambers to exterminate large numbers of people, especially Jews. People were herded into a sealed room into which poisonous gas was pumped. Four gas chambers were located at Auschwitz. Gas chambers were also operated at Majdanek and five other concentration camps in German-occupied Poland. By the end of the war, 6 million Jews and millions of others deemed undesirable had been murdered by Nazi Germany.

example of Lloyd George at the end of World War I by going to St. Margaret's Church. With his fingers in the sign of a *V*, Churchill walked out on the balcony and said:

> *God bless you all. This is your victory! It is the victory of the cause of freedom in every land. In all our long history we have never seen a greater day than this. Everyone, man or woman, has done their best. Everyone has tried. Neither the long years, nor the dangers, nor the fierce attacks of the enemy, have in any way weakened the independent resolve of the British nation. God bless you all.* [5]

Churchill was overjoyed that Germany had been defeated. But his elation would be short-lived. Three months later, he would suffer a defeat that would be one of the greatest disappointments of his life. ⌐

In London, the crowd cheers Churchill and his cabinet as they appear on the balcony of the Ministry of Health building on May 8, 1945.

Winston Churchill gives his famous wartime victory sign.

Sir Winston, Farewell

On July 26, 1945, the results of Britain's general elections were finally known. Churchill was confident he would win, but the Labour Party won by a landslide. Churchill would still be a member of Parliament as head of the

Conservatives, but there would be a new prime minister: Clement Attlee.

Britons were grateful to Churchill, but their votes proved they wanted another government to manage postwar recovery. Churchill was devastated by the loss. That summer, he attended his last official war meeting—the Potsdam Conference—where decisions for the postwar world were made. But the war was not yet over; Japan had not surrendered.

On August 6, 1945, U.S. President Harry Truman ordered an atomic bomb to be dropped on Hiroshima, Japan. Three days later, a second atomic bomb was dropped on Nagasaki, Japan. On August 14, the Japanese accepted terms of surrender offered by the Allies. Much of the world celebrated on September 2—V-J (Victory over Japan) Day— when Japan formally surrendered. World War II was over.

Gifts to Churchill

Winston Churchill received gifts from sovereigns and dignitaries all over the world. From Spain, he received the head of a famous bull; the creature had been dedicated to Churchill by the bullfighter who killed it. From Switzerland, he received a clock that never needed winding. Jamaica gave him 500 cigars, and Cuba gave him 10,000. He received a kangaroo from Australia and an ebony walking stick from South Africa. His most famous gifts were Rota the lion and Sheba the leopard, which he often visited in London Zoo.

Postwar Years

Churchill was determined to be Britain's prime
minister again. In the meantime, he busied himself
with writing and hobbies. Between 1945 and 1951,
he wrote five of the six volumes of his history of the
war, *The Second World War*. At Chartwell, he farmed
and built fishponds, barns, and stables. He also
painted. He vacationed with Clementine in France,
Switzerland, Morocco, and Madeira. In March
1946, Churchill delivered a famous speech about the
division of Europe at Westminster College in Fulton,
Missouri. He described an iron curtain that divided
free Western Europe from the Soviet
Communists and their satellites.

Return to Harrow

In one of his speeches to
the students at Harrow
School, Churchill said,
"[T]his is the lesson: never
give in, never give in, never, never, never, never—in
nothing, great or small,
large or petty—never give
in except to convictions of
honour and good sense.
Never yield to force; never yield to the apparently
overwhelming might of
the enemy."[1]

Prime Minister Again

In 1951, the Conservative Party
returned to power, and 76-year-
old Churchill was once again prime
minister of Great Britain. He
worked as tirelessly as ever until heart
problems returned and he had to
cut his workload. He thought about
retiring but convinced himself to stay
active. He was determined to bring

the United States, Great Britain, and the Soviet Union to a summit conference.

In 1952, King George VI died. Queen Elizabeth II succeeded her father to the throne. One of her first acts as queen was to confer on Churchill the high distinction of naming him a member of the Most Noble Order of the Garter. King George VI had offered Churchill the Garter at the end of World War II, but Churchill refused because of his recent political defeat. He quipped, "I could hardly accept His Majesty's offer of the Garter when his people have given me the Order of the Boot."[2] He accepted the honor in 1953 and became Sir Winston.

Every year, Churchill visited Harrow. The school honored the man who had achieved so much and risen to international acclaim. When Churchill arrived in 1953, students and staff cheered. Together, they sang Churchill's favorite songs. The schoolboys added a final verse to one of his favorites:

And Churchill's name shall win acclaim/From each new generation:/

For you have power in danger's hour/Our freedom to defend, Sir!/ Though long we fight we know that right/We triumph in the end, Sir![3]

DECLINING HEALTH

The years ahead of Churchill were filled with
health problems. In June 1953, newspapers reported
that he was overworked and had to reduce his
commitments. However, he had suffered a severe
stroke that paralyzed one side of his body and left
him unable to speak. Churchill's condition was
concealed from the public. This was not his first
stroke—the first occurred in 1949—but this one was
the worst. Doctors were not sure he would survive,
but the 78-year-old was not yet ready to give up the
fight. He gave himself four months to recover.

Churchill was taken to Chartwell, where he
regained the ability to speak. He scoffed at the
wheelchair that was provided for him. In a few
weeks, he learned to sit up again, grasp things with
his hands, stand, and take steps. By September, he
was walking, talking, and mingling with the public.
Again, he had fought and won.

But Churchill's physical and mental faculties
declined. Fellow members of Parliament encouraged
him to resign from politics. On April 4, 1955,
Queen Elizabeth II was Churchill's guest at a
farewell dinner at 10 Downing Street. The next day,
Churchill resigned his position as prime minister of

*Winston Churchill's eightieth-birthday portrait,
taken at 10 Downing Street*

Great Britain. Out of respect, the Queen waited two
days to appoint his successor, Sir Anthony Eden—
something that had never been done before.

On April 7, 1955, Churchill left the prime
minister's residence for the last time. Outside,
people cheered for him. Churchill nodded in

thanks, put a cigar in his mouth, and held up two fingers in the distinctive *V*. He then got into a car that took him home to Chartwell.

LIFE AFTER POLITICS

In his retirement, Churchill enjoyed many of the things he loved most: writing, racehorses, and painting. And he remained in Parliament, which had been such a huge part of his life since 1901. He visited the House of Commons often, sitting in a corner seat on the center aisle that was respectfully reserved for him. But now it was different—he sat silently and just listened.

In his last years, Churchill reflected on his dual heritage. He completed and published the four-volume *A History of the English-Speaking Peoples*, which he had begun before the war. One volume was about the early history of the United States. In 1959, Churchill accepted an invitation from President Dwight D. Eisenhower to visit the United States. It was his fifteenth visit to the United States since his first visit in 1895.

Churchill's Thoughts on Death

Churchill met death the same way he had lived life—fearlessly. He was once asked if death held any terror for him. In his typical witty fashion, he replied, "I am prepared to meet my Maker. Whether my Maker is prepared for the great ordeal of meeting me is quite another matter."[4]

He was glad to be in the land where his mother was born and to visit a people with whom he had such a strong bond.

A Man to Honor

Churchill received many awards throughout his life. He was presented with France's Cross of Liberation and the Nobel Prize for Literature. In his eighties, he was given honorary citizenship in three countries. In April 1963, Congress made 88-year-old Churchill the first honorary citizen of the United States. Churchill was too weak to travel to

Honorary Citizen of the United States

When Randolph Churchill accepted the honorary citizenship of the United States bestowed upon his father by President Kennedy, he spoke words written by his father:

I have received many kindnesses from the United States of America, but the honour which you now accord me is without parallel. I accept it with deep gratitude and affection. . . .

I am, as you know, half American. . . . In this century of storm and tragedy I contemplate with high satisfaction the constant factor of the interwoven and upward progress of our peoples. Our comradeship and our brotherhood in war were unexampled. We stood together, and . . . the free world now stands.

Mr. President, your action illuminates the theme of unity of the English-speaking peoples, to which I have devoted a large part of my life. I would ask you to accept yourself, and to convey to both Houses of Congress, and through them to the American people, my solemn and heartfelt thanks for this unique distinction, which will always be proudly remembered by my descendants.[5]

Washington DC to accept the award. He sent his
son in his place. On April 9, 1963, on television,
Churchill heard President John F. Kennedy's words
of respect and admiration:

> We meet to honor a man whose honor requires no meeting—
> for he is the most honored and honorable man to walk the
> stage of human history in the time in which we live. Whenever
> and wherever tyranny threatened, he has always championed
> liberty. . . . Indifferent himself to danger, he wept over the
> sorrows of others. A child of the House of Commons, he
> became in time its father. . . . Now his stately Ship of Life,
> having weathered the severest storms of a troubled century, is
> anchored in tranquil waters, proof that courage and faith and
> the zest for freedom are truly indestructible. The record of his
> triumphant passage will inspire free hearts for all time.[6]

CHURCHILL DIES

On January 10, 1965, 90-year-old Churchill
suffered a massive stroke and fell into a coma. He
died on January 24. His father had died on that
same day 70 years earlier.

Churchill was given a state funeral. Queen
Elizabeth II attended Churchill's funeral, as did
numerous sovereigns and heads of state from all

Winston Churchill with his wife, Clementine, on his ninetieth birthday

over the world. His body was placed in famous
Westminster Hall, part of the House of Parliament,
for mourners to pay their respects. The state funeral
continued to St. Paul's Cathedral with a funeral
service that was seen by tens of millions of people on
television. His body was then taken to the Tower of
London. There, it was taken up the Thames River

to Waterloo Bridge on a barge. From there, a train took the coffin to St. Martin's Church near Churchill's birthplace at Blenheim Palace. Sir Winston Leonard Spencer Churchill was buried at Bladon Churchyard next to his father, mother, and brother. ⌐

Eisenhower's Farewell

As Churchill's body was taken up the Thames, Dwight D. Eisenhower—former World War II general, former president of the United States, and Churchill's dear friend—spoke:

"At this moment, as our hearts stand at attention, we say our affectionate, though sad, goodbye to the leader to whom the entire body of free men owes so much. . . . May God grant that we—and the generations who will remember him—heed the lessons he taught us: in his deeds, in his words, and in his life. May we carry on his work until no nation lies in captivity; no man is denied opportunity for fulfillment. And now, to you Sir Winston—my old friend—farewell!"[7]

A statue of Winston Churchill keeps watch over Parliament.

TIMELINE

1874	1882–1893	1893
Winston Leonard Spencer Churchill is born on November 30 in England.	Churchill attends boarding school at St. George's School for boys, the Misses Thomson School, and Harrow School.	Churchill enrolls in the Royal Military Academy at Sandhurst.

1899	1900	1905
In October, Churchill serves as war correspondent in South Africa. He is taken prisoner, escapes, and joins the army to fight as a soldier.	Churchill is elected to the House of Commons.	Churchill is appointed to his first ministerial post: undersecretary of state for the colonies.

1895

In February, Churchill is commissioned as second lieutenant of the Fourth Hussars.

1896

Churchill is stationed in India with the Fourth Hussars.

1898

Churchill's first book, *The Story of the Malakand Field Force,* is published.

1908

Churchill marries Clementine Hozier on September 12. He is appointed Board of Trade president and begins a period of social reform.

1910

Churchill is appointed home secretary and made responsible for Britain's prisons.

1911

Churchill is appointed first lord of the admiralty and put in charge of the Royal Navy.

Timeline

1914

The Great War (World War I) begins on August 1, and Churchill mobilizes the Royal Navy.

1917

Churchill is appointed minister of munitions, making war munitions for Britain and the United States.

1918

Churchill is appointed secretary of state for war and air and put in charge of Britain's army and air force.

1940

Churchill is appointed prime minister and minister of defense of Great Britain on May 10.

1945

On July 26, Churchill loses his position as prime minister.

1951

Churchill becomes prime minister for a second time.

1921	1924	1939
Churchill is appointed secretary of state for the colonies.	Churchill is appointed chancellor of the exchequer and put in charge of Britain's finances.	Great Britain declares war on Germany on September 3. World War II begins; Churchill is again appointed first lord of the admiralty.

1953	1955	1965
Churchill is named a member of the Most Noble Order of the Garter by Queen Elizabeth II on April 24.	Churchill resigns as prime minister on April 5.	Churchill dies on January 24.

Essential Facts

Date of Birth

November 30, 1874

Place of Birth

Blenheim Palace, Oxfordshire, England

Date of Death

January 24, 1965

Parents

Lord Randolph Churchill and Jennie Jerome Churchill

Education

St. George's School, the Misses Thomson School, Harrow School, and the Royal Military Academy at Sandhurst

Marriage

Clementine Hozier (1908)

Children

Diana, Randolph, Sarah, Marigold, Mary

CAREER HIGHLIGHTS

Churchill served in the military and was a published author before beginning his political career. He continued as a soldier and author after becoming a politician. While a war correspondent in South Africa, he was taken prisoner, and then escaped. Churchill was first elected to Parliament in 1900. He held different roles in British government, including being in charge of the Royal Navy and Britain's finances. He was appointed prime minister of Great Britain twice. Churchill's finest hour came during World War II. He helped avert Britain's defeat in 1940 and saw the war through to victory.

SOCIETAL CONTRIBUTION

As a member of Parliament and British prime minister, Churchill worked for social reform, including old-age pensions and unemployment insurance for Britons. As leader during World War II, his decisions affected innumerable people worldwide, especially by helping bring the war to an end. As an author, his many works have enlightened readers about war, politics, culture, and freedom.

CONFLICTS

As a soldier, Churchill fought in India and Africa. As a politician, he faced numerous opponents in British Parliament. As prime minister, his greatest foe was Adolf Hitler.

QUOTE

"I have nothing to offer but blood, toil, tears and sweat. . . . You ask, what is our policy? I can say: It is to wage war by sea, land and air, with all our might and with all the strength God can give us; to wage war against a monstrous tyranny, never surpassed in the dark, lamentable catalogue of human crime. That is our policy.

You ask, what is our aim? . . . It is victory, victory at all costs, victory in spite of all terror, victory, however long and hard the road may be; for without victory, there is no survival."
—*Winston Churchill, House of Commons, London, May 13, 1940*

ADDITIONAL RESOURCES

SELECT BIBLIOGRAPHY

Best, Geoffrey. *Churchill and War*. London: Hambledon and Continuum, 2005.

Churchill, Winston S. *My Early Life: A Roving Commission*. London: Thornton Butterworth Limited, 1930.

Churchill, Winston S. *The Second World War*. The Gathering Storm. Wilmington, MA: Mariner Books, 1986.

Gilbert, Martin. *Winston Churchill's War Leadership*. New York: Vintage Books, 2003.

Severance, John B. *Winston Churchill: Soldier, Statesman, Artist*. New York: Clarion Books, 1996.

FURTHER READING

Adams, Simon. *Winston Churchill*. New York: Raintree Steck-Vaughn Publishers, 2003.

Gilbert, Martin. *Churchill and America*. New York: Free Press, 2005.

Gilbert, Martin. *Winston Churchill: The Wilderness Years*. Boston: Houghton Mifflin, 1981.

Macdonald, Fiona. *Winston Churchill*. Milwaukee, WI: World Almanac Library, 2003.

WEB LINKS

To learn more about Winston Churchill, visit ABDO Publishing Company online at **www.abdopublishing.com**. Web sites about Winston Churchill are featured on our Book Links page. These links are routinely monitored and updated to provide the most current information available.

Places to Visit

Blenheim Palace

Woodstock, Oxfordshire OX20 1PX, United Kingdom
+44(0) 1993 811091
www.blenheimpalace.com
Winston Churchill's birthplace and burial place, the palace features
2,100 acres (850 ha) of formal gardens, a magnificent lake, and
an exquisite palace with furnishings and paintings that belonged
to Churchill's ancestors, the dukes of Marlborough, and some of
Churchill's paintings.

Chartwell

Mapleton Road, Westerham, Kent TN16 1PS, United Kingdom
+44 1732 868381
Chartwell was Winston Churchill's home from 1924 until his
death. Today, its rooms and gardens are much the same as they were
during Churchill's life. Many of Churchill's paintings can be
viewed in the garden studio.

Churchill Archives Centre

Churchill College, Storey's Way, Cambridge CB3 0DS,
United Kingdom
+44 1223 336087
www.chu.cam.ac.uk/archives
The organization houses Winston Churchill's personal papers and
the archives of 570 other people, documenting the history of the
Churchill era and after.

Churchill Museum and Cabinet War Rooms

Clive Steps, King Charles Street, London SW1A 2AQ,
United Kingdom
+44 (0)20 7930 6961
cwr.iwm.org.uk
Exhibits trace the exciting story of Winston Churchill, including
his World War II years and his private life.

GLOSSARY

ally
> A country that is united with another, especially during war.

armistice
> A temporary stop of fighting by mutual consent; a truce.

besieged
> Surrounded by enemy forces.

cavalry
> Troops fighting on horseback.

cipher system
> Code or a method of secret writing.

coalition
> The coming together of separate individuals or groups temporarily to work toward a cause or action.

Communism
> A system intended to be based on common ownership of property; the political system of the Soviet Union.

concentration camp
> A camp where civilians, enemies, or political prisoners are confined, almost always under cruel conditions.

cryptographic
> Pertaining to cryptography, or secret writing.

dissidents
> Those who disagree with established policy.

flogging
> The beating or whipping of, such as with a stick.

infantry
> Soldiers trained to fight on foot.

meningitis
> A disease in which the membranes covering the brain and spinal cord swell.

Parliament
    The British legislative body; it is made up of the House of
    Lords and the House of Commons.

rearmament
    To equip again with weapons, usually in preparation for war.

regime
    A government in power.

reparations
    Payment required from a defeated nation for damages done by
    the defeated nation during a war.

strait
    A narrow channel joining two larger bodies of water.

suffragette
    A supporter of women's right to vote.

U-boat
    A German submarine, the word is short for *Unterseeboot*,
    a German word meaning "undersea boat."

war correspondent
    A journalist assigned to report directly from a war zone.

warmonger
    One who attempts to create conflict.

Source Notes

Chapter 1. Prophet of Truth

1. Winston Churchill. *Never Give In!: The Best of Winston Churchill's Speeches.* New York: Hyperion, 2003. 101.
2. Martin Gilbert. *Churchill: A Life.* New York: Henry Holt and Company, 1991. 511.
3. Adolf Hitler. "Speech of September 16, 1930." Munich, Germany. 8 Jan. 2008 <http://www.hitler.org/speeches/09-16-30.html>.
4. Winston Churchill. "Blood, Toil, Tears and Sweat." House of Commons, London. 13 May 1940. *The Churchill Centre.* 8 Jan. 2008 <http://www.winstonchurchill.org/i4a/pages/index.cfm?pageid=391>.
5. Winston Churchill. "Their Finest Hour." House of Commons, London. 18 June 1940. *The History Place: Great Speeches Collection.* 8 Jan. 2008 <http://www.historyplace.com/speeches/churchill-hour.htm>.

Chapter 2. Young Winston

1. Winston S. Churchill. *My Early Life: A Roving Commission.* London: Thornton Butterworth Limited, 1930. 17.
2. Winston Churchill. *My Early Life: 1894–1904.* New York: Touchstone, 1958. 10.
3. Martin Gilbert. *Churchill: A Life.* New York: Henry Holt and Company, 1991. 20–21.
4. William Manchester. *The Last Lion: Winston Spencer Churchill: Visions of Glory 1874–1932.* Boston: Little, Brown and Company, 1983. 160.

Chapter 3. Military Training

1. Winston S. Churchill. *My Early Life: A Roving Commission.* London: Thornton Butterworth Limited, 1930. 34.
2. William Manchester. *The Last Lion: Winston Spencer Churchill: Visions of Glory 1874–1932.* Boston: Little, Brown and Company, 1983. 209.
3. Martin Gilbert. *Churchill: A Life.* New York: Henry Holt and Company, 1991. 39–40.
4. Ibid. 40
5. Ibid.

6. Winston S. Churchill. *My Early Life: A Roving Commission*. London: Thornton Butterworth Limited, 1930. 19.

7. Winston S. Churchill. *My Early Life: A Roving Commission*. London: Thornton Butterworth Limited, 1930. 74.

Chapter 4. Soldier, Journalist, Politician

1. Mary Soames, Ed. *Winston and Clementine: The Personal Letters of the Churchills*. New York: Houghton Mifflin Company, 1998. 16.

Chapter 5. The Great War

1. Martin Gilbert. *Churchill: A Life*. New York: Henry Holt and Company, 1991. 275.

2. Mary Soames, Ed. *Winston and Clementine: The Personal Letters of the Churchills*. New York: Houghton Mifflin Company, 1998. 97.

3. Martin Gilbert. *Winston S. Churchill: Volume Three: The Challenge of War: 1914–1916*. Boston: Houghton Mifflin Company, 1971. 473.

4. John Lukacs. *The Duel: The Eighty-Day Struggle between Churchill and Hitler*. Princeton, CT: Yale University Press, 2001. 38–39.

Chapter 6. Wilderness Years

1. Martin Gilbert. *Churchill: A Life*. New York: Henry Holt and Company, 1991. 465.

2. Martin Gilbert. *Churchill and the Jews: A Lifelong Friendship*. London: Simon and Schuster, 2007. 99.

3. Winston S. Churchill. *The Second World War: Volume One: The Gathering Storm*. Boston: Houghton Mifflin Company, 1986. 109.

4. Winston Churchill. *Never Give In!: The Best of Winston Churchill's Speeches*. New York: Hyperion, 2003. 181–182.

Chapter 7. World War II

1. Winston S. Churchill. *The Second World War: Volume One: The Gathering Storm*. New York: Houghton Mifflin Company, 1948. 61.

2. Ibid.

3. Winston Churchill. "Blood, Toil, Tears and Sweat." House of Commons, London. 13 May 1940. *The Churchill Centre*. 8 Jan. 2008 <http://www.winstonchurchill.org/i4a/pages/ index.cfm?pageid=391>.

4. Ibid.

Source Notes Continued

5. Winston Churchill. "We Shall Fight on the Beaches." House of Commons, London. 4 June 1940. *The Churchill Centre*. 8 Jan. 2008 <http://www.winstonchurchill.org/i4a/pages/index.cfm?pageid=393>.

Chapter 8. The Battle of Britain
1. Gilbert, Martin. *Churchill: A Life*. New York: Henry Holt and Company, 1991. 675.
2. Winston Churchill. "A Dark and Deadly Valley." House of Commons, London. 22 Jan. 1941. *The Churchill Centre*. 8 Jan. 2008 <http://winstonchurchill.org/i4a/pages/index.cfm?pageid=388>.
3. "The Very Model of a Democratic Statesman." *The Churchill Centre*. 8 Jan. 2008 <http://www.winstonchurchill.org/i4a/pages/index.cfm?pageid=714>.
4. "The End of the Beginning." *The Churchill Society London*. 4 Dec. 2007. <http://www.churchill-society-london.org.uk/EndoBegn.html>.
5. Winston Churchill. "This is Your Victory." Ministry of Health, London. 8 May 1945. *The Churchill Centre*. 8 Jan. 2008 <http://www.winstonchurchill.org/i4a/pages/index.cfm?pageid=427>.

Chapter 9. Sir Winston, Farewell
1. Winston Churchill. "Never Give In, Never, Never, Never." Harrow School, London. 29 Oct. 1941. *The Churchill Centre*. 8 Jan. 2008 <http://www.winstonchurchill.org/i4a/pages/index.cfm?pageid=423>.
2. "FAQs — Politics." *The Churchill Centre*. 8 Jan. 2008 <http://www.winstonchurchill.org/i4a/pages/index.cfm?pageid=434>.
3. Winston Churchill. *Never Give In!: The Best of Winston Churchill's Speeches*. New York: Hyperion, 2003. 306.
4. "Their Finest Hour." The Churchill Centre. 13 Feb. 2008 <http://www.winstonchurchill.org/i4A/pages/index.cfm?pageid=601&textonly=1>.

5. Winston S. Churchill. Sir Winston's response to being named an honorary citizen of the United States as read by Randolph S. Churchill. The White House, Washington, DC. 9 April 1963. "Citizen of the United States" *The Churchill Centre*. 8 Jan. 2008 <http://www.winstonchurchill.org/i4a/pages/index.cfm?pageid=430>.

6. John F. Kennedy. Remarks to Churchill's honorary citizenship. The White House, Washington, DC. 9 Apr. 1963. "Citizen of the United States" *The Churchill Centre*. 8 Jan. 2008 <http://www.winstonchurchill.org/i4a/pages/index.cfm?pageid=430>.

7. John G. Plumpton. "The Funeral of Sir Winston S. Churchill." *The Churchill Centre*. 8 Jan. 2008 <http://www.winstonchurchill.org/i4a/pages/index.cfm?pageid=803>.

INDEX

ABOUT THE AUTHOR

Sue Vander Hook has been writing books for more than 15 years. The focus of her writing career is educational books for children and young adults. She especially enjoys writing about historical events and biographies of people who have made a difference in the world. Sue lives with her family in Minnesota.

PHOTO CREDITS

Corbis, cover; Keystone/Corbis, 6; AP Images, 9, 15, 16, 55, 65, 70, 77, 83, 95; Michael Nicholson/Corbis, 22; Bettmann/Corbis, 25, 31, 39, 43, 89; Hulton-Deutsch Collection/Corbis, 26, 33, 56, 66, 74, 84, 93; J.E. Purdy/Corbis, 34; Red Line Editorial, 44, 50, 73; Bettman/Corbis/Churchill Heritage Ltd., 52; Ludovic Maisant/Corbis, 60